The Bluffer's®
Guide to
Accountancy

Liz Fisher
John Courtis

Oval Books

Published by Oval Books

Telephone: +44 (0)20 7733 8585
Fax: +44 (0)20 7733 8544
E-mail: info@ovalbooks.com
Web site: www.ovalbooks.com

Published by Ravette Publishing, 1987
Reprinted/updated: 1989,1991,1992,1993,1994
1995,1996,1997,1998

Published by Oval Books, 1999
New edition 2004; updated 2006
New edition 2008

Series Editor – Anne Tauté

Cover designer – Vicki Towers
Cover image – Aris Multimedia Entertainment Inc., 1991-3
Printer – Liberdúplex, Spain
Producer – Oval Projects Ltd.

The Bluffer's® Guides series is based
on an original idea by Peter Wolfe.

The Bluffer's Guide® , The Bluffer's Guides®,
Bluffer's®, and Bluff Your Way® are
Registered Trademarks.

ISBN: 978-1-906042-58-5

CONTENTS

INTRODUCTION

It has been said that an accountant is someone who solves a problem you didn't know you had in a way you don't understand. Accountancy, as a profession, has surrounded itself with an air of mystery and confusion that excludes the ordinary mortal and leaves a lucrative stream of income for those who are left. This confusion is generated by the belief that accountancy's complex concepts can only be understood by qualified accountants and other people who know how to add. Bluffers therefore need to be armed with enough knowledge to indicate that they could, if they wished, explode the myth.

> 66 Becoming a qualified accountant takes years of study, hard work and cheap suits. 99

So this book is for those who know nothing about accountancy, but feel they ought to; those round the fringes of accountancy who need to know a little more but are deterred by the mystique, and those in accountancy who feel just a little insecure about their grasp of the total picture. This covers quite a lot of people.

Becoming a qualified accountant takes years of study, hard work and cheap suits. It is not our intention to turn you into an imitation accountant; such a transformation would be highly undesirable, if not actionable. Instead, we offer you a basic grounding in the principles and language of accounting, which will enable you to mingle freely with accountants and finance staff without being spurned as a rank outsider.

A superficial overview of accountancy and a repertoire of questions relevant to the places where accountancy touches the real world, like reporting, forecasting and client relationships, will be quite sufficient to convey the impression that you know what the answers should be, and where the slush fund is hidden.

THE BASICS

Accounting comes in many forms, from the scribbled notes about household income and outgoings to an inch-thick, glossy annual report produced by a multinational organisation. Even though the two documents may appear to be miles apart, the basic principles (and, some would argue, the amount of useful information contained in each) remain the same.

Knowledge of these fundamental principles will get a bluffer far, however painful it may be to learn them. The sensible approach would be to adopt the view taken by thousands of trainee accountants before you; short term pain means long-term gain. In their case the end result is an impressive salary and the occasional risk of social embarrassment. Bluffers, of course, can read on in the superior knowledge that their intention is to flit confidently through the world of the accountant and never to become one.

Book-keeping

The most important thing to remember about book-keeping is that there are no books. There used to be. Accountancy was once a deeply pleasing process of entering transactions neatly into columns, adding, subtracting and ticking. Everyone knew where they stood. And then some bright spark invented a computer and it all began to go horribly wrong.

> 66 The most important thing to remember about book-keeping is that there are no books. 99

The 'book' part of 'book-keeping' used to mean the ledgers – huge, satisfying books that contained almost all the information an accountant needed to know. These are now are a dying phenomenon. Ledgers are still used in some small businesses, but the computer-generated equivalent that is used by the vast majority of businesses today resemble a traditional ledger as closely as *Dirty Dancing* resembles an in-depth sociological study of the American teenage psyche. Still, for the sake of thoroughness, if not nostalgia, we will continue.

There are several species of ledger. The most important, and the largest, is the Nominal Ledger. All other ledgers should, in theory, reconcile to a control account in the nominal ledger. In the good old days the nominal ledger would be recognisable as a massive, leather-bound object that commanded instant respect among finance staff. Today, it will be part of a computer programme. In either case, though, the easiest way to make an accountant cry is to pretend that you've lost it.

> **❝ The easiest way to make an accountant cry is to pretend that you've lost the nominal ledger. ❞**

The Personal Ledger contains the accounts of suppliers and customers, subdivided into Bought (or Purchase) Ledger and Sales Ledger. These list the trade creditors and debtors of the business.

Each page of the sales ledger is generally divided into two, with debits (i.e., invoices issued) on the left and credits (cash received) on the right. The normal case of affairs in a sales ledger is for the debits to exceed the credits since, as any small business owner will tell you, collecting money from customers is like getting blood out of a stone.

A Private Ledger is somewhat archaic and is only used by businesses that are so secretive that they want to hide part of the nominal ledger away from the peasants. In this sort of business, the employees are the peasants.

The computer age

The invention of spreadsheet software packages has had much the same effect on the accountancy profession as the invention of the calculator had on the standard of school mathematics. Since pupils have been allowed to take calculators into maths exams, few have shown an ability to add two and two without resorting to pushing buttons. Similarly, there is a perception that the younger

> **66** Many older accountants, while they can claim to understand the mechanics of accounting, still need help to switch on their mobile phone. **99**

generation of qualified accountants know what a spreadsheet looks like, but wouldn't know one end of a ledger from the other. This is why older accountants tend to view younger, I.T.-literate accountants with barely-disguised contempt, in the same way that those of us who used pencils and logarithm tables in school view the calculator generation. What the bluffer should remember is that this contempt serves to hide a much deeper insecurity since many older accountants, while they can claim to understand the mechanics of accounting, still need help to switch on their mobile phone.

Because so many spreadsheet software packages that are available on the retail market are aimed at non-accountants, the spreadsheet cannot be claimed by the accountancy profession as a mysterious tool that only qualified (and expensive) accountants can understand. As a result, qualified accountants now tend to deal in enormously complex spreadsheets – the bigger and more complex, the better. In fact, accountants have been known to spend a disproportionate amount of time comparing the relative size of their spreadsheets. This is just one reason why you should think very carefully before inviting an accountant to a dinner party.

> **66 Accountants have been known to spend a disproportionate amount of time comparing the relative size of their spreadsheets. 99**

The advent of the spreadsheet means that almost no-one, including recently qualified accountants, understands the underlying processes of accounting. The universal availability of spreadsheets may have delivered to the masses the ability to produce beautifully presented figures in tabular form, but few people now appreciate that any relationship between what is presented and the underlying reality relies on the skill of the author (or in some cases accident, but you will come to that later).

For the purposes of bluffing, it is not necessary to worry about detailed book-keeping techniques. Assume the methods work and, like the innards of your personal computer, do not meddle with them. However, it is useful to recognise the language of basic accounting in order that you can change the subject and move on to higher things when they crop up.

Single entry book-keeping

Single entry book-keeping, as the name suggests, involves entering the details of each transaction once. Each case of expenditure is recorded listing the date, the amount and the payee. Similarly, cash received is also written down. Hundreds of tiny organisations and organised householders detail their transactions in this way today, as do all of the major banks – a bank state-ment is the best example of single entry book-keeping you are likely to see.

> **" A bank statement is the best example of single entry book-keeping you are likely to see. "**

Single entry may seem entirely logical – it is, after all, a waste of energy and paper to write most things down twice – but, as will be seen, single entry book-keeping has been quickly eclipsed by its devilishly clever brother, double entry book-keeping. Single entry book-keeping is, in fact, the accountancy equivalent of getting into a wheelbarrow when the man next door is firing up his top-of-the range Jaguar.

Double entry book-keeping

This simple arithmetical idea is the nub of modern accounting and is based around the concept that every transaction involves the giving of a benefit and the receiving of a benefit. There are two rules to double entry book-keeping:

1 Debit on the left, credit on the right. Traditionally, debits are on the left hand side of the books of account (ledgers) and the credits on the right hand except on a traditional Balance Sheet, where the reverse applies to confuse the enemy. (All non-accountants are the enemy, by the way.)

2 For every debit there must be a credit. In other words, for every entry on the debit side (generally representing assets, expenses incurred or losses) there must be a numerically identical entry on the credit side of another account (representing liabilities, revenues or shareholders' funds, including profits).

The main advantage of the double entry system is that it's very easy to spot if something has gone wrong, because the two sides – the debit and credit sides, for those who are paying attention – should balance.

Trainee accountants will learn the basics of double entry book-keeping on their first day, which involves drawing a ledger or account (a big 'T', in effect), for each entry. Debits appear on the left of the T, credits on the right. Accounts clerks used to be told, incidentally, that debits go on the side nearest the window until someone realised that that only applies if all accounts clerks in the world sat with the window to their left, or indeed, near a window at all.

> **❝The main advantage of the double entry system is that it's very easy to spot if something has gone wrong, because the two sides should match. ❞**

To get the basics of double entry book-keeping, you only need to look at a simple example. Mrs S runs a bookstore. One morning a customer comes in and buys £100 worth of books, for which he pays with a cheque. She records the transaction as follows:

Sales	
	£100 (credit)

Bank account	
£100 (debit)	

Easy-peasy. You're practically an accountant already. Now assume the customer wishes to buy £100 worth of stationery which attracts VAT. The customer would, as a result, pay £117.50 for the stationery (£100 for the goods plus VAT at 17.5%). The transaction would be recorded:

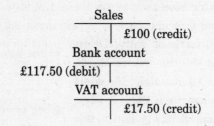

Sales
| £100 (credit)

Bank account
£117.50 (debit) |

VAT account
| £17.50 (credit)

Both sides, as you can see, balance.

To make it a little more tricky, say Mrs S decides to extend her shop, so she takes out a loan for £20,000 from her bank, secured against her house. The following day, she pays a builder a deposit of £2,000 for the work and a customer buys £100 of books. Another customer buys £200 of stationery on credit. A third buys a biro for 89p and shoplifts a gold-plated business card holder worth £250. The day after that, Mrs S's house burns down and the builder demands an extra £7,000 on top of his estimate. He also wants to be paid the balance in euros, so Mrs S takes out a 3-year foreign exchange hedge to protect herself against any changes in the exchange rate.

This example amply illustrates the drawback of double entry book-keeping; that nothing in life is that simple.

The trial balance

It should be instantly apparent that if all the double entries in the book are correct, not only will they mean something but the net balances in each account will, when listed, balance left against right in total. Quite often, due to human error, they do not. Hence the need for a Trial Balance, which can be done at any point to check whether the arithmetic is wrong.

This obsession with the possibility of error pervades the whole history of accounting and may explain why the few exams needed for entry to accountancy training (until recently) included compulsory mathematics.

> **The obsession with the possibility of error pervades the whole history of accounting.**

If you wish to imply massive familiarity with the process of assembling accounts at a year end, you must think yourself into the long hours spent poring over a trial balance which does not balance, and know a few of the reasons why it does not.

Additions, as hinted above, are a classic cause. More subtle are transpositions. All differences divisible by nine probably result from a transposition. For example, an error of £6,300 tells you that someone has recorded £7,000 at one end of the transaction and £700 at the other.

The same applies with, for example, £879.12 which to the experienced eye is divisible by 99 and therefore must be a sum recorded in pounds on one side and pence on the other – in this case £888.00 and £8.88. Auditors punch-drunk with fatigue often miss this and you can look terribly good if you just look at all such differences for the 9 and 99 factors.

> **66** Accountants have been known to spend a disproportionate amount of time comparing the relative size of their spreadsheets. **99**

Omissions are another – i.e., a single entry without a balancing opposite number. Look through the ledgers for the exact amount of the difference. Just one lucky diagnosis of this sort and your reputation is made.

The uncertainties of double entry

Double entry book-keeping, when properly practised, can be a deeply satisfying experience. Nothing gives a trainee accountant a feeling of joy quite like the credit and debit sides balancing on the first attempt. It is only a little later that they learn that a balance does not necessarily mean that the accounts are arithmetically correct or that they portray a true result. Of the many possible reasons for this, you need only know two.

The first is that if the data is being processed by a formal accounting software package, the arithmetical truth remains credible. However, if the data is in the form of a print out from some other programme, even a spreadsheet, the arithmetical certainty is less certain or altogether absent.

> **If someone inventive can make a loss or an expenditure appear to be an asset, the whole picture will seem better.**

The other problem is that each side of the books has several groups of accounts in it. They are unrelated and differ in principle and effect. For instance, most will include the following types of balance:

Debit (left side)	Credit (the right)
* assets	* liabilities
* expenditure	* revenues
* losses	* profits
	* provisions and reserves

It follows logically that if someone inventive can make a loss or an expenditure appear to be an asset, the whole picture will seem better. Similarly, so will the subtle transformation of reserves or liabilities into revenues, thus later increasing profits or at least reducing losses. This is known as creative accounting or fiddling, depending upon your point of view. To indulge in creative account-ing is considered a Bad Thing, particularly if you are caught.

The task of spotting the difference between legitimate creative accounting (sometimes referred to as 'brilliance'), disallowable creative accounting (sometimes known as 'unlucky') and fiddling (always known as fiddling) falls on the auditor.

66 Auditors are not necessarily expected to spot if one of their clients has strayed too far into creative territory. 99

At least, that is what many people believe. The truth is that auditors are not necessari-ly expected to spot if one of their clients has strayed too far into creative territory. This is one of the most-controversial areas of accounting so the topic will be revisited a little later, when you've had a cup of tea.

The accounts

Now that you have grabbed the basics of double-entry book-keeping, it is time to move on to the finished article – the company accounts. In every case this will consist of the two most important documents:

1 the balance sheet
2 the profit and loss account.

The profit and loss account shows the revenue and expense for a particular period; the balance sheet shows what is left.

The balance sheet

The Balance Sheet is a summary of balances at the end of a particular period, grouped into fairly intelligible generic headings which together provide a snapshot of the financial state of the organisation at that point. Bluffers should call it a 'snapshot' because this trivialises the thing and distracts attention from its imprecision. The most important points to remember about a Balance Sheet are implicit in its name; it should balance, and, er, it is presented on a sheet of paper.

> **Bluffers should call it a 'snapshot' because this trivialises the thing and distracts attention from its imprecision.**

The balance sheet shows the company's assets and liabilities, the difference between the two representing the capital account (the money invested in the business by the owners). This assumes, incidentally, that assets exceed liabilities. If the liabilities exceed the assets the company has no net worth and should not, in theory, be trading. Many do, however, supported by friendly bankers and personal guarantees.

Technically, it would be more informative to call

the balance sheet a 'statement of assets and liabilities' but the uncertainty about whether it would actually balance took precedence over the real meaning of the document during its formative years. Do not remind accountants of this point. They know only too well that unless the accounts are computerised and therefore arithmetically correct (although potentially meaningless in other respects) the major panics in auditing and accounting are still about getting the books to balance and look meaningful, rather than about taking action as a result.

> 66 Unless the accounts are correct, the major panics in auditing and accounting are still about getting the books to balance and look meaningful, rather than about taking action as a result. 99

Until fairly recently, the two elements of the balance sheet – assets and liabilities – were laid out side by side. This caused some confusion, as was noted before, since assets (debits) appeared on the right hand column and liabilities (credits) on the left, disobeying the basic rule of double-entry and confusing several generations of trainee accountants. It is normal practice today to list assets and liabilities vertically, showing liabilities deducted from assets.

At this point we regret you are going to have to learn to read a balance sheet; not perfectly, but well enough for the uncertainty implicit in all balance sheets to cover the rest of your ignorance. This uncertainty is not just the result of the arithmetical worries mentioned earlier. By the time outsiders see a balance sheet it is virtually certain to balance.

The problem now arises from the fact that nearly all the figures on it are in some way philosophically suspect. Knowing how and why they might be wrong is more useful than knowing about high accounting principles.

The assets

The assets are normally arranged according to the ease with which they can be turned into ready money. Money is the most liquid asset – this is easy to remember for anyone who spends it. Fixed assets, land and buildings for example, are the least liquid.

> **66 Money is the most liquid asset – this is easy to remember for anyone who spends it. 99**

On the conventional balance sheet the **fixed** assets come first, probably to impress the bank manager. These are the assets whose use generates benefit to the business in the long term (usually taken to mean more than one year) and include buildings, plant and machinery, vehicles, computers, furniture and things with some degree of permanence.

The uncertainty at this level is that the fixed assets are rarely worth the amount listed in the balance sheet. Business is required by accounting conventions and good practice to provide for depreciation over the working life of the asset on a fairly arbitrary basis. Depreciation is the loss in value that an asset suffers from age, or use, or both. The rate of depreciation varies for different types of assets. In the case of a new car, it is well known that the vehicle depreciates by approximately one third of its value in the first 10 feet it progresses from the dealer's door.

> **❝ It is well known that a new car depreciates by approximately one third of its value in the first 10 feet it progresses from the dealer's door. ❞**

The arbitrary nature of depreciation is best illustrated by the example of an office building. Depending on its position, its architectural value and the state of the property market, a building could well appreciate dramatically over time. Even so, accounting convention dictates that it should be depreciated. The result is that a building that could be sold for £575,000 is booked in the balance sheet as worth £2.99. Clearly, this is not good accounting.

The profession's answer to this conundrum was the introduction of the concept of fair value, which essentially means that an accountant can ascribe any value he or she likes to an asset, as long as they can convincingly argue to an auditor that they are more or less correct. Which, given the attention span of the average auditor, is not particularly difficult.

Current assets, assets whose value is available to the business in the short term, are easier. These include stock (inventory, if you are American, or are talking to one), trade debtors (receivables), cash and bank accounts, and short-term investments. They may all be

> **"**An accountant can ascribe any value he or she likes to an asset, as long as they can convincingly argue to an auditor that they are more or less correct.**"**

called current assets, but they have wildly different degrees of liquidity. 'Stock', for instance, may include raw materials, work in progress and the finished product. The last of these is the most marketable and therefore the most liquid.

Accountants have another word for the more liquid current assets. They are known as 'quick assets' because they can be realised fairly promptly. Stock does not fall into this category; cash does, as, for some unfathomable reason, do debtors. Anyone who has tried to get money out of a debtor may beg to differ.

Now it gets complicated. There is a third category of assets, one that you cannot feel, or touch, but which may be worth millions. These are **intangible** assets. The most common intangible asset is goodwill, which is essentially the difference between the price paid for a company and the value of its assets. This difference caused enormous confusion in the profession until someone identified goodwill as the value of customer loyalty, brands, staff expertise and the other engines that drive a successful business.

66 How to deal with goodwill has occupied the profession for years, but the generally accepted view is that the figure should be capitalised. 99

How to deal with goodwill has occupied the profession for years, but the generally accepted view is that the figure should be capitalised (i.e., its current value is estimated and booked in the balance sheet) and then written off over time through the profit and loss account, so recognising that the goodwill you have bought has a finite and reducing value. To the non-accountant, the fact that you have:

- paid more for something than the sum of its tangible worth,
- called that overpayment an asset, and then
- destroyed the value of that asset in an arbitrary manner over a set amount of time,

may seem bizarre. To most accountants, however, it is entirely reasonable.

Another important intangible asset for several very large conglomerates is the brand. A few companies carry brands on their balance sheet that are

worth several hundred million pounds. Whether they are worth several hundred million pounds in reality, of course, is a highly debatable point.

Intangible assets are a particularly complex area, for even an accomplished bluffer. Fortunately, FRS 10, the accounting standard (there are standards, surprisingly) dealing with goodwill and other intangible assets, is an appallingly long text so a dismissive reference to its 'unnecessary verbosity' should convince both accountants and amateurs that you have actually perused it yourself.

> **“A dismissive reference to FRS 10's 'unnecessary verbosity' should convince both accountants and amateurs that you have actually perused it yourself. ”**

The liabilities

There are two types of liabilities; **current** liabilities and **long-term** liabilities. Current liabilities are those that a business could be called upon to pay off in the short term, such as trade creditors, bank overdrafts and taxation. Long-term liabilities are those that are due after more than one year. Accountants in business spend a significant proportion of their time finding ways of making as many liabilities as possible long-term liabilities, since this eases the pressure on the company's working capital.

Just to confuse, liabilities are arranged in descending order of liquidity. In other words, it starts with the things that are likely to be paid soonest – which is taken to mean within a year – and goes on to those that are likely to be paid later.

One of the first items to appear will be creditors' accounts (otherwise known as payables). Modern accountants have brought to a fine art the technique of using this as an essential part of the working capital of the business. They do not like having attention drawn to this.

> **When dealing with a slow-paying company, it is important to remember that they will always be prepared to pay a determined creditor in preference to a weak one.**

Trade creditors are those customers that the company is trying to fob off with excuses. The higher the figure, the more successful the company at stalling. Late payment has become part of normal business practice, so when dealing with a slow-paying company, it is important to remember that they will always be prepared to pay a determined creditor in preference to a weak one, particularly if the determined creditor's armoury includes the threat of liquidation.

Strangely, the really hardened late payers are not offended by the many stalling tactics employed by companies. They regard the juggling act as a game and actually admire good technique. One masterly financial director of a distinguished but insolvent television company spent a year fending off creditors and only paying against the documentation which would have had the company wound up. Even writs were a licence to delay. One creditor complained that the accounts payable system was not working, only to be advised that it was working perfectly, but its objectives were somewhat different from the norm.

Long term liabilities start with loan capital, which pays interest to the investor and will normally have to be repaid eventually. Long term loans, perhaps secured on mortgage, come next, followed by deferred liabilities (like future tax arising from past profits).

> **"The apostrophe is particularly misleading since it suggests that the equity belongs to the shareholders."**

The amount that is left after all liabilities have been deducted from all assets is called the shareholders' equity. The apostrophe is particularly misleading since it suggests that the equity belongs to the shareholders. Technically, it does, but in reality the shareholders cannot get hold of it until the company or business is wound up (and even then, they are unlikely to see much of it).

The profit and loss account
If you have any difficulty with the balance sheet, there is good news and bad news. The bad news is

that the profit and loss account makes the balance sheet look relatively simple, since the balance sheet deals mainly in ascertainable facts. By comparison, the profit and loss account (or the p&l account, as it is known) is much closer to fiction. The good news is that, while the p&l account is less certain in its content, the experts get confused too.

The p&l account is a summary of all the revenue and expenses that have occurred during a particular time period, most usually one year. For that reason, a p&l account that is not headed and dated will be as pointless as selecting George W. Bush as your phone-a-friend on *Who Wants to Be a Millionaire?*

66 When the affairs of a business are hopelessly confused the accountants carry out two balance sheet audits. 99

The main aim of the p&l account is to show the profit (or loss) the company has made during the accounting period. This sounds simple, but it is not. Profit can be a complicated business.

What accountants tend not to tell others is that when the affairs of a business are hopelessly confused the accountants carry out two balance sheet audits – one at the beginning of the period and one at the end. The difference in the company's net worth between the two dates is the profit (or loss) for the period. All of the complex data in the p&l account boils down to this simple fact. If the net worth of the business has increased in the period, there is a profit. A decrease means a loss. All the accounting flim-flam in the world cannot conceal this. Even so, the accountant has to come up with a reasonably convincing argument to produce the same figure in the p&l account.

Beginning from the top, a correctly produced p&l account will show a turnover figure, less cost of sales, leading to a gross profit figure.

Everyone usually agrees that the 'cost of sales' figure is necessary because it includes only the direct costs and expenses that are clearly necessary to the generation and sale of the product or service. You can't sell an omelette without buying some eggs (unless you own chickens, which would be known as vertical integration and is quite beyond our present brief) so everyone accepts the cost of the eggs as 'direct'. It is the downward progression, from the gross profit to the final pre-tax figure, which causes most internecine strife within companies.

Most trading accounts show a profit. You have to be fairly dim or very unlucky to give away products or services so cheaply that the trading account shows a loss. However, the body of the p&l account deducts from this gross profit all the expenses that

You can't sell an omelette without buying some eggs (unless you own chickens), so everyone accepts the cost of the eggs as 'direct'.

the production people regard as luxuries rather than essentials. For the production staff, the ideal world is one where the customers come to the factory gate, buy what the factory happened to make that day, pay in cash and come back the next day for more.

Unless you are running a stall selling free range eggs at the farm gate this dream is seldom realised. There are nuisances like accountants, directors, sales staff, marketing staff, personnel staff, buildings to house them in, advertising expenses, distribution costs, bank charges, audit fees, legal fees and security guards. All these at certain times can seem like non-essentials.

> **People in charge of the various cost centres fight bitterly over accepting fringe items into their particular slice of the accounts.**

Traditionally, this is an area that causes internal strife within companies as the people in charge of the various cost centres which bear these costs fight bitterly over accepting fringe items into their particular slice of the accounts. But that's their problem. Everyone else will be concentrating on the 'bottom line' figure in the p&l account. The real skill lies in identifying the bottom line. It is not necessarily, as its name suggests, the last line to appear in the p&l account. Sometimes it is the figure that companies would like us to believe is its profit figure.

For many listed companies, this is the pre-tax profit figure, the number normally reported in their six-monthly performance announcements. But this ignores the fact that the company has no choice but to pay a sizeable chunk of its profits to the taxman, so the figure that is actually available to the company and its shareholders is considerably less than the pre-tax figure. It is rather like saying that you have £50 in your wallet when you know full well that you owe £20 to a mobster who will break your fingers if you don't pay up.

> **It is rather like saying that you have £50 in your wallet when you know full well that you owe £20 to a mobster who will break your fingers if you don't pay up.**

NB: the provision (meaning the estimate) for taxation will almost invariably be a conservative one. No auditors are going to sign a set of accounts which understates the possible tax burden arising, but they will all quite happily sign against the maximum provision and then let the tax department work like hell to avoid paying that figure. Only if they and the company get their sums or their principles wrong will the full amount, or any greater one, be paid.

There are, in fact, a number of other unavoidable expenses that a company may have to pay that appear below the pre-tax profit figure in the p&l account. These are known as 'below the line' items and accountants work hard to put as many expenses as possible into this category. Until recently, the most popular of these was 'extraordinary items'.

Much to the chagrin of business, though, the accounting regulators have stamped on this practice and now the only item that could be considered extraordinary is a spaceship landing on the High Street. Companies' response to this is to label some items 'exceptional', which means that they can appear below the profit figure. These items are rarely that exceptional.

A question of size

Companies of all sizes will produce a balance sheet and profit & loss account as a minimum, but the general rule to remember is that the size of a company is directly proportionate to the size of its annual accounts. It is also true that the size of the annual accounts is inversely proportionate to the amount of useful information contained therein.

66 The general rule to remember is that the size of a company is directly proportionate to the size of its annual accounts. 99

In general, think of the distinction between then accounts of small and large companies in terms of the difference between children and adults. Small businesses sometimes need a lot of help in order to produce anything useful (or indeed recognisable to the average human being) and their accounts will inevitably be eclectic, chaotic and noisy. Large company accounts by contrast are professional, well-groomed and expensive, but get beneath the surface and you may find all sorts of nastiness.

It is also important to remember that the contents of the final accounts depend very much on the needs and prejudices of the intended readership. The accounts of small businesses are generally only meant for the bank manager and the taxman, which means that they have a very particular slant (and are written in large type with words of one syllable). The bank manager will lend the business money on the strength of the accounts and the tax man will take money away. Everything, therefore, rests on the income figure and on the assets the business owns.

66 Think of the distinction between the accounts of small and large companies in terms of the difference between children and adults. 99

The accounts of large companies, on the other hand, are meant for a very different audience – current and potential shareholders, journalists and analysts. These accounts will be glossy, long and contain many words of three syllables or more. This does not mean that they are more comprehensive than a small company's accounts, or that the reader is more intelligent. It merely means that the company is hoping to impress those who are impressionable, and confuse those who are not.

Small company accounts

Often, the accounts of small businesses do not resemble accounts at all. Ask to see the purchase or sales ledger and you will be pointed towards a filing cabinet that, when opened, spews out thousands of crumpled receipts and invoices like confetti.

> **Ask to see the purchase or sales ledger and you will be pointed towards a filing cabinet that, when opened, spews out thousands of crumpled receipts and invoices like confetti.**

In a small business, it is important to remember that everything revolves around cash; how much the business has, how much it is making, how much the owner has. For this reason the cash book will be one of the most important documents. Remember, though, that in most businesses the cash book does not record cash in hand. It only records sums in the bank account (unless the business actually trades in cash, as with a retail store). The only cash on the premises is recorded in the petty cash book, or the owner's wallet (which is almost the same thing).

Most businesses actively dislike cash these days because it represents a security problem. Those who do like it are generally small traders who like to be able to take money out of the till and feel they are cheating the tax man.

Dealing mainly in cash does have its dangers and if you are talking to a small business owner, or are considering buying a small cash business such as a pub, shop or restaurant, there is one invaluable piece of information to remember. Invariably, the present proprietor will always point to two comfort factors in the accounts:

1 The way business is improving.

2 The fact that the real profits are higher than those shown in the books because he or she has been taking several hundred pounds per week or month out of the cash takings.

Be warned. The most likely scenario is that the business appears to be improving because the former illicit drawings are now being left in the till to create an apparent improvement in the closing months. The true picture is, therefore, that you are being asked to pay for a non-existent trend and non-existent excess receipts.

Worse, if the business is a limited company and you buy the company, you are liable for the past fiddles when the tax authorities eventually catch up. Hire a good accountant.

Large company accounts

The mainstay of the language of analysts is the ratio analysis, a range of numbers that sound impressive but are in fact merely numbers taken from the accounts and divided by other numbers taken from the accounts. This enables analysts to make definitive statements about the performance and health of the company, and lots of money.

The main ratio that current shareholders of a company are concerned with is the eps figure, which essentially tells them in a nutshell how well the company is doing with their money. A good eps figure means that everyone is happy. A poor eps result means that shareholders get cranky and eventually, highly-paid heads will roll. Connected to eps is the price/earnings ratio (the current market price of a share, divided by earnings per share). The ratio effectively measures the number of years it will take (at the current rate of eps) for an investor to get his money back, but the general rule is that companies with a high P/E ratio tend to be a better investment bet in the future than those with a low

> **66** A good eps figure means that everyone is happy. A poor eps result means that shareholders get cranky. **99**

P/E ratio.

In the accounts of listed companies the balance sheet and profit and loss account play a small but essential supporting role in a cast of thousands. The published accounts of listed companies (known as the annual report and accounts) are a devilishly dense document packed (at first glance) with information, only a fraction of which will be of any use or interest. Along with plenty of pictures, the final published accounts of a listed company will contain a myriad of tables, reports and narratives, including:

Consolidated profit and loss account and balance sheet

Consolidated accounts bring together several sets of final accounts belonging to several companies that are all part of the same group, often in several currencies. This is the accountancy equivalent of three-dimensional chess. Good consolidation accountants are god-like creatures in their own field. They tend to stay in it.

Cash flow statement

The cash flow statement tells you how and why the cash (or overdraft) shown in the balance sheet has changed during the year. It is the one statement that it is not easy to manipulate and therefore one

of the best indicators of how a company is perform-
ing. The exception is any company that seems to be
generating a great deal of cash in currencies that
you have never heard of.

Statement of total recognised gains and losses

These are not actual gains or losses in the real,
money sense, but gains or losses that do not show
up in the p&l account, things like revaluations,
currency gains or losses or prior-year adjustments.
Prior-year adjustments are mistakes that were
made in last year's accounts that have to be cor-
rected in this year's accounts.

The chairman's statement

An opportunity for the company chairman to
repeat any good news, while skating over bad.
While the report is signed by and plastered with
misty portraits of the chairman, it is extremely
unlikely that he actually wrote it. Public relations
departments are much better qualified for the task
and besides, a remarkable number of company
chairmen cannot spell.

Directors' report and/or operating and finan-
cial review

Usually a chief executives report and/or the finance
directors' report. Long an unutterably tedious, it is

often worth reading carefully because if there is any bad news, it will be buried in the middle of the longest paragraph.

Report of the independent auditors

An opportunity for the auditors to say that the accounts are 'true and fair' while stressing that the company could be riddled with fraud for all they know, or care.

Corporate governance report

An opportunity for the company to pat itself on the back for the independence of its executives and the thoroughness of its processes.

Directors' remuneration report

By far the most interesting part of any annual reports and accounts, this sets out the size of senior executives' pay packet in black and white, for all to see. Embarrassment about the size of some of these packets has led many companies to split 'remuneration' into many components, including pension payments, share options and expense allowances. Don't be fooled, just add the figures together.

Notes to the accounts

The most dense and impenetrable and also the

most informative section of the accounts. The figures in the balance sheet and profit and loss statement when read alone mean very little. The workings that explain how the company arrived at the figures in the balance sheet and p&l account will appear in the notes, along with plenty of extremely useful information, from a detailed list of exactly where a company earned its income, to how much the auditors are paid. Any experienced reader will always begin any set of accounts with the notes, since that is where all the critical information, and any bad news, will be hiding.

> 66 The workings that explain how the company arrived at the figures in the balance sheet and p&l account will appear in the notes, along with plenty of extremely useful information. 99

How to read a set of accounts

Annual reports and accounts are intended to impress wealthy but intellectually challenged shareholders (or potential investors) and others who believe that a lot of words and figures equates to useful information. So it is as well to know how to handle, 'read' and discuss a set of accounts. The basic formula is as follows:

- Pick up the document, tut at its weight and mutter about trees and the environment.

- Turn immediately to the Notes to the Accounts and pretend to be absorbed for as long as it takes for anyone to notice.

- Find the Directors' Remuneration section and read out a figure, any figure (they will all be large). Tut again.

- Turn to the profit & loss statement and read the bottom line, just in case someone asks.

- Throw it away.

In many situations, this is all you will ever need. If you find yourself in a situation where a little more is demanded than the apparent appearance of competence, the quickest and most effective route is to take a page out of the analysts' book and use a ratio.

Ratios are an invaluable tool for bluffers since the results

66 A handful of key ratios scattered into a conversation give the impression that you are accountancy literate. 99

sound impressive and it is not necessary to understand any of the underlying processes, or even the words. A handful of key ratios scattered into a conversation give the impression that you are accountancy literate and understand a company's finances completely. This will be especially impressive because while many accountants can add, relatively few know how to divide.

The most frequently used ratios are:

Current ratio
This ratio (current assets divided by current liabilities) is a good measure of a company's liquidity, or its ability to pay its debts. If the figure is above 2, the company is in good shape. If it is below 1, run for the hills.

Quick ratio
This is very similar to the current ratio but excludes stock from current assets on the basis that it can be difficult to sell quickly. The assets that are left, debtors and cash, can be sold quickly. Hence the name. This isn't rocket science.

Gearing ratio
Debt divided by equity. This figure indicates the level of nervousness of the company's bankers, on a percentage scale.

Return on equity
Profit before tax divided by equity. This figure indicates the happiness of the shareholders, on a percentage scale.

Return on Capital Employed (ROCE)
This ratio (operating profit divided by net operating

assets) is the ultimate measure of an organisation's
financial performance. It does, however, depend on a
bluffer being able to recognise the relative figures in a
balance sheet and p&l statement, so should only be
used in an emergency.

Fixed asset productivity
Sales divided by fixed assets. This is largely meaningless but it is unlikely that anyone will notice.

A guide to auditing

All companies above a certain size must have their
accounts audited every year. The statutory audit is
the bread and butter of the accountancy profession.
Audits are like funerals. They are necessary but
no-one actually wants to have one, except accountants and undertakers.

The annual audit involves a number of stages:

1 The company asks a number of accountancy
   firms for a quote for the work.
2 The senior partners of a number of firms spend
   at least an hour each explaining to the company's executives how useful an audit can be, how
   thorough their staff are, and how important the
   client is to them.
3 The company chooses the cheapest firm.
4 Two teenagers from the auditing firm turn up at

the company, two days earlier than expected.

5   They spend several days asking daft questions.

6   The firm signs off the accounts.

7   The firm sends an enormous invoice to the company.

The purpose of an audit is to confirm to shareholders, investors and other users of the company's accounts that the accounts represent a 'true and fair view' of its financial position. This is not necessarily true, as the accounts could suggest that the company is doing well when thanks to a fiendishly complicated fraud carried out by one or more of its executives, in reality it is close to collapse.

66 It is not fair that the auditors should be expected to uncover a fraud. Auditors are watchdogs, not bloodhounds. 99

But it is not fair that the auditors should be expected to uncover a fraud. This is a cause of some confusion and distress among companies, since they often misguidedly believe that if they are required to pay a firm of auditors to check their accounts annually, they should expect the auditors to discover any financial dodgy dealings. The auditing profession argues that a determined fraudster has, by definition, fooled the company and so will probably lie to the auditors as well. And auditors are not lie detectors. They are watchdogs, not bloodhounds, and a fraud is the responsibility of the company alone. Which may be true, but it's certainly not fair.

This is an explosive area (or, at least, as explosive as the accountancy profession gets). It is important for a bluffer to remember that an accountant's view of the audit will depend on whether he or she works for an audit firm or for a company. When speaking to an auditor, it makes sense to be:

a sympathetic about the need for an audit and

b supportive about what an audit is for.

When speaking to an accountant in business it makes sense to be:

a sympathetic about the cost of an audit and

b supportive about the absolute pointlessness of it all.

If you ever find yourself in conversation with both an auditor and an accountant in business it makes sense, if only for your own amusement, to introduce the subject of the annual audit and then stand well back.

The limitations of an audit and the respective responsibilities of the auditor and the company's directors are clearly spelled out in every step of the process. When a firm of auditors is engaged to a company it sends an audit engagement letter, which sets out the terms of the contract and makes it clear that the role of the auditor is not to detect fraud. The annual reports and accounts will also state at length the responsibilities of the directors when it comes to fraud and good stewardship, and

❝Over 90% of the audit report sets out the responsibilities of the auditors in completing the audit. The important bit comes at the end.❞

stress that the directors are entirely responsible for the contents and accuracy of the accounts. None of this will prevent a suit against the auditors, however, if something goes wrong.

At the end of the audit process the auditing firm will issue an audit report, which is reproduced in the annual report and accounts. Over 90% of the report sets out the responsibilities of the auditors in completing the audit. The important bit comes at the end, under 'audit opinion'. This will say that the firm believes that the accounts represent a 'true and fair' view of the state of the company's affairs at that date. If it says anything else, even something you don't understand, something is very seriously wrong indeed.

Creative accounting

At this stage it may be helpful to consider why proprietors seek to manipulate the accounts.

**People want to improve the balance sheet
because:**
   a it will impress bankers, suppliers and credi-
      tors with an illusion of greater solvency.
   b it is an automatic by-product of improve-
      ments to the profit figures.

People want to worsen the balance sheet:
   a usually as a by-product of the conservative
      accounting necessary to lower profit figures
      (see below), or
   b to facilitate a management buy-out at a
      depressed price.

**People want to improve the profit figures in
the p&l account to:**
   a protect the directors' reputations or bonuses
   b assist a sale at a firm price
   c deter a bid at the wrong price
   d cover fraud.

People want to worsen the profit figures to:
   a minimise the tax bill
   b hide profits from non-director shareholders
   c hide profits from the unions
   d hide excess profits from customers, particu-
      larly governments, who take a particularly
      dim view of this, whether or not cost-plus
      contracts are involved.

Given these reasons, which can seem very compelling to the people involved, it is not surprising that from time to time a large example of creative or conservative accounting slips past even the best auditors.

> **66** Auditors are not too worried about conservative accounting. Anything the directors do which makes it likely that the net worth of the company is understated gives them great comfort. **99**

Another trade secret about auditors is that they are not too worried about conservative accounting. Anything the directors do which makes it likely that the net worth of the company is understated gives them great comfort. They know to their own and their insurers' cost that accountants generally get sued when the assets are deficient, not when they are in surplus. Unless they suspect a company is engaged in a massive tax evasion exercise, anything less is tolerable, particularly if debated on a high moral plane beforehand.

There is another reason for this. Auditors usually have little confidence in the audit process and suspect there may well be an unintentional overvaluation elsewhere, even when the directors are busy undervaluing stock, debtors and anything else in sight. The known undervaluation reduces the chances that the unknown will sneak up on them later.

Other known reasons why there could always be trouble ahead include:

- the assumption that computerised accounts must be right. This is a fiction for two reasons. First, balancing numerically does not prove that the accounts tell the truth. Second, computerised accounts only balance on paper if programmed to do so. Fraud, incompetence and bugs can all prevent this.

- the extraordinary scale of modern business and thus the potential for honest error, to say nothing of the other kind.

The other kind

Creative accounting sits firmly in the twilight zone. In the tax field there is a clear distinction between tax evasion, which is illegal, and tax avoidance, which is both legal and respectable (and expensive, if you can find someone who can do it properly). The borders around creative accounting are less clearly defined. Generally, creative accounting is the subtle manipulation of

> 66 In the tax field there is a clear distinction between tax evasion, which is illegal, and tax avoidance, which is both legal and respectable (and expensive). 99

assets, liabilities, provisions and other figures in order to improve the apparent net worth of a company and/or its profits. The line between creative accounting and brilliant technique is ever changing. The most dramatic shift in the line comes immediately after an accounting scandal, when it becomes apparent that a billion-dollar organisation with an apparently healthy balance sheet is actually worth slightly less than a bag of peanuts. For a short while, everyone agrees that creative accounting is a Bad Thing, but this rarely lasts long.

Creative accounting divides the profession as starkly as the Sean Connery/Roger Moore question divides fans of James Bond. In general, accountants in industry (the preparers of accounts) spend their lives pushing the boundaries of accounting technique well into the creative wasteland. Auditors, by contrast, spend their lives frowning at creative accounting while desperately trying not to upset the client too much before they are able to send out their invoice.

❝ Creative accounting divides the profession as starkly as the Sean Connery/Roger Moore question divides fans of James Bond. ❞

The job of stamping out the worst excesses of creative accounting lies with the national accounting standard setting body in each jurisdiction, and the International Accounting Standards Board internationally. The rules that allowed the bad kind of creative accounting have been tightened up, but there is still some room for manoeuvre for the dishonest, the determined and the down-right foolhardy.

> **66** Interpret the rules in a way that inflates turnover or reduces expenses and – boom – you have creative accounting. **99**

In principle, creative accounting is very simple indeed and relies entirely on the fact that the annual profit figure is, to a large extent, subjective. The final figure will depend on a series of interpretations of accounting rules. Interpret the rules in a way that inflates turnover or reduces expenses and – boom – you have creative accounting. Whether it is allowable accounting or deliberately misleading is a question, ultimately, for the auditors. This is known as passing the buck.

A convincing bluffer should have a few examples of creative accounting to call upon in an emergency:

Dodgy deliveries

There are many ways of booking sales into a particular financial year, even though the transaction is technically not completed during that year. You could, for instance, deliver to a customer on a sale-or-return basis, or deliver in one financial year and

47

specify that the customer does not have to pay for the goods until the following year. Unscrupulous companies could even deliver a product that does not work properly, and then fix it in the following financial year. In each case, the transaction is booked prematurely, which inflates turnover temporarily.

Backdated invoices

The polar opposite of dodgy deliveries. Goods are not supplied before the year-end but the invoice is backdated to appear that they were.

Capitalising expenses

This involves company executives convincing themselves that when they have spent a large sum of money on something that may generate money in the future but which has no physical presence, they have, in fact, created an asset. They have not. They have reduced retained profits or reserves. It is rather like spending £1 on a lottery ticket and then convincing everyone that you are worth £9m for the next week.

Endless depreciation

If an asset has a natural life of 10 years but you choose to depreciate it over 20, the depreciation charge in the accounts will be half of what it should be for each of those 20 years, which will reduce expenses and boost profits. The downside is that this is a short-term fix – after 10 years the company will be stuck with a depreciation charge that it would not otherwise have. But by then, the company may be out of trouble, or bust, so no-one will care.

The indestructible asset

The rules say that if a company owns an asset that becomes obsolete, because of new developments in technology or because the Human Resources Director spilt a cup of coffee over it, the value of the asset should be written off in the current year's accounts. Since that puts a hefty dent in the current year's profits, companies will often look for increasingly desperate arguments to justify why the asset is still in everyday use, perhaps as a hat-stand.

> **❝ Provisions allow you to make largely judgmental reductions or increases thereby increasing or decreasing profits. They can also, with skill, be reversed. ❞**

Provisions

Provisions are the accountant's friend and an incredibly versatile tool. They allow you to make largely judgmental reductions or increases in, say, trade debtors, thereby increasing or decreasing profits. They can also, with skill, be reversed. So, if a company has made higher profits than analysts were expecting in a particular year, an increase in a provision can reduce profits to something nearer expectations. The following year, when profits are not so healthy and analysts are blindly optimistic, the provision is reversed on the basis that last year's provision was too high. Profits go up and everyone is happy.

Revenue recognition

The general rule in the kitchen is that it's not wise to eat something before it's thoroughly cooked. The opposite applies with revenue – recognising revenue before it is technically revenue is an excellent way of boosting profits and has the added benefit that it does not cause salmonella. Dodgy deliveries (q.v.) are probably the best-known example of creative revenue recognition.

How to spot creative accounting

Many auditors can spend an entire career failing to spot creative accounting that is going on under his or her own nose, so no bluffer could be expected to spot dubious accounting practices. Even so, there are a number of warning signs that could indicate that a company is not everything that it seems:

- The company has 'weak internal controls'. This usually means that the audit committee meets once every six months, in a pub.
- The audit partner is crying.
- The chief executive and chairman of the company is the same man, and he owns a big yacht.
- The non-executive directors are all related to the chief executive. And they all own yachts.

THE FANCY BITS

Accountants can be a sensitive bunch and it is remarkably easy to upset them. One of the worst criticisms of their profession is that it is essentially backward-looking in that it records and checks what has already happened in a business. This implies that accountants only exist to check the work of much more pro-active people.

> **“One of the worst criticisms of accountancy is that it is essentially backward-looking in that it records and checks what has already happened. ”**

A particular breed of accountants, though, do deal with forward-looking information. These tend to be accountants in business, such as management accountants. Fewer still reach the upper echelons of the profession and deal in company strategy. These accountants at the 'cutting edge' of business (in so far as accountancy has an edge) try to disassociate themselves from their ticking and bashing counterparts.

66 **Management accountants in particular feel somewhat superior to other kinds of accountants, especially chartered accountants.** 99

Management accountants in particular feel somewhat superior to other kinds of accountants, especially chartered accountants working in practice who spend their lives checking other people's information and telling them that it's wrong. Even so, chartered accountants tend to look down on management accountants.

The distinction between accountants in practice and those in industry is rather like directions on a map. An accountant will tell you where you have been and, reasonably accurately, where you are now (unless someone has maliciously removed the road signs, or has turned them around, in which case it's not their fault that you are lost). The accountants covered in this section tell you where you are going and, more importantly, how to get there.

Management accounting

A management accountant produces daily, weekly and monthly information that is used in the strategic decision-making of his or her organisation. Management accountants are a breed apart. They train, qualify, and spend their lives working in industry, producing solidly useful, forward-looking information that people can use to make decisions that actually take them somewhere.

You may feel that management accounting implies accounting for management. There is some misunderstanding on this point. What managers say they want from accountants is 'information'. This is a code word meaning (depending on the managers and the circumstances): solutions, ratio analyses, ideas, decisions, good news, recommendations, panaceas, excuses, culprits, therapy, whitewash or moral support.

The misunderstanding arises because few managers tell their accountants that the word 'information' is, in fact, code. Fewer tell them which code is in use this week. In conse-

> **❝ The misunderstanding arises because few managers tell their accountants that the word 'information' is, in fact, code. ❞**

quence, if they are lucky, managers may get information. If they are not lucky they just get plain old-fashioned accounts, which to the average accountant are management information at its best.

Management accounts are an accountant's view of what management wants. Unless they are received and improved by strong non-financial managers, they may be useless, or worse.

The other important point to remember about management accounts is that they are usually wrong. (The word 'wrong' should never be applied to management accounts in public. The preferred phrase is that you are 'unhappy with the figures'.) The errors are usually the result of variances – otherwise known as life getting in the way of estimates. In most businesses, the variances tend to be unfavourable. This is because people outside and inside the business are much more likely to generate accidental costs and expenses than to find 'windfall' revenues. The prime characteristic of a windfall, as Sir Isaac Newton found, is that it raps you smartly on the occiput and, unless you want to discover gravity, this comes as an unpleasant surprise.

> **" The errors are usually the result of variances – otherwise known as life getting in the way of estimates. "**

It follows that reporting against budgets will throw up some of these variances (which leads the company to exceed the expense budget) and omit some (which come as a nasty shock later when the financial accounts are compared with the management accounts).

Integrated accounts

It is often alleged by an organisation's accountants that the financial accounts are wholly integrated with and derived from the management accounts. This is another myth.

One of the main reasons why accountants in commerce and industry go into a deep depression just before and just after the end of the financial year is that this is the time when the chickens come home to roost and it becomes apparent even to the meanest intellect that there is a yawning gulf between the real figures (the books of account, which lead via the financial accounts to the annual statutory report) and the figures on which management has been relying for the past 11 months.

> **One of the main reasons why accountants in commerce and industry go into a deep depression just before and just after the end of the financial year is that this is the time when the chickens come home to roost.**

Now we come to the trade secrets: the reasons why all accountants know the figures are likely to be wrong, although this realisation retreats readily to their subconscious mind and appears to come to them quite fresh whenever the facts emerge.

This is a golden opportunity for a bluffer to gain ill-deserved respect and it should be grabbed with gusto. Seek out the company's analysts – the people with the task of analysing the management and financial accounts and reconciling the two. The magic formula is to ask for their help in one specific area of analysis. Go to them after a month in which the organisation has done particularly well according to the preliminary figures and ask, nay insist, that they investigate the reasons for the favourable variances. This will usually come as a surprise to them.

The average investigative team is likely to be sitting on its collective butt breathing a quiet sigh of relief and waiting for the next crisis. They will want to know why you are interested. It is permissible to tell them, because when you are proved right (this is a win/win deal – you will always be right) you will look omniscient.

66 The magic formula is to ask for their help in one specific area of analysis. 99

There are three standard reasons for favourable variances between the preliminary figures and actual performance figures:

1 The possibility that too much revenue has sneaked into the period's accounts. This is usually a calendarisation error, which means the sum involved should have been in the previous period – or the next one.

2 The equally strong possibility that a significant chunk of costs or expenses has been omitted.

Again, it will be in the wrong period, previous or subsequent, unless there is a backlog in the accounts-payable function and someone's desk drawer is stuffed with unprocessed invoices from suppliers. Fortunately this cannot happen at the revenue end, unless someone on a profit-related bonus has noticed that this period is crucial for bonus purposes and has massaged the revenue figures (difficult, often fraudulent, but not impossible).

3 (A more worthy cause), you want to know the real reason why it was such a good month, so that the organisation may be equipped and motivated to repeat the effort. (This always wins.)

Points (1) and (2) will not astound the analysts, although they will kick themselves if they had not thought of them first. The third will often do so. Analysts spend so much time analysing that they have little or no time to go out and influence management to do something with the figures. The idea that they might venture forth with good news, demanding a repeat performance, is likely to strike them as so radical that they prefer to delegate upwards or

> 66 Analysts spend so much time analysing that they have little or no time to go out and influence management to do something with the figures. 99

57

sideways – to the Controller, or even to you.

Analysts never forget that in olden days the messenger who brought bad news frequently lost his head. The principle still applies, aggravated by the fact that this sort of company has senior managers who cannot tell good news from bad unless it is colour-coded or explained to them very slowly and in words of one syllable.

> 66 Analysts never forget that in olden days the messenger who brought bad news frequently lost his head. 99

You must remember that nearly all the things noted above which could cause favourable variances can happen in reverse and generate unfavourable ones. It is not necessary to list all the variances in the accountant's knapsack but a gentle catalogue of questions exploring the possibilities can be guaranteed to unsettle both accountants and managers whose areas are in the spotlight, for two reasons:

1 The possibility that you could by accident be right.

2 The suspicion that since you obviously know the questions to ask, you may know something about the underlying facts that they don't know.

Budgets

A budget is an annual, monthly, or weekly plan of the financial progress of a business. It is important that you are fluent in the vocabulary of budgeting and are aware how imperfect budgets can be, and why. This largely relieves you of the obligation to take them seriously. It will also reduce the risk that you will be asked to compile them. Very few managers, financial and other, are likely to entrust the articles of their faith to a known atheist. You do not invite a pacifist to play cowboys and indians.

Do not be overawed by budgets. There are so many ways of presenting them, and compiling them, that they look complex and authoritative. They are not.

The key reason you can always sneer at budgets, even if you were a party to them, is that most accountants tend to generate budget information and then fail to obtain agree-

> **It is important that you are aware how imperfect budgets can be, and why. This largely relieves you of the obligation to take them seriously.**

ment from management for the full budget package which results. In consequence even the least numerate 'broad brush' managers who could look at the totals and know instinctively that they are rubbish, do not have the chance to do so before the year is well under way, by which time it is better to keep quiet. They can blame the budget development process later, when actual results look sick.

The ugly truth is that the actuals always prove the budgets wrong. (Always call the actual results 'the actuals'.) The massive authority generated by the sophisticated compilation process is eroded as soon as the first few months of the year have passed and flaws are visible. It is at this point that managers suddenly become numerate and point knowingly to all the weaknesses they kept quiet about in the first place. They know, better than most accountants, that budgets can never be perfect. Unlike most accountants, they have no professional belief in their innate rightness. This gives them a clearer view.

> **66 The ugly truth is that the actuals always prove the budgets wrong. (Always call the actual results 'the actuals'. 99**

Budgets go wrong in three ways, which is useful to know when both preparing and reading a budget:

1 The revenues are exaggerated because no-one wants to be a prophet of doom at the beginning of the year, when everyone is feeling unreasonably optimistic. Sales people in particular view budgets as targets to be aimed for, rather than best estimates of likely performance. Their bonus target, on the other hand, is seen as a target that must be hit at all costs, even if they have to run over their own granny on the way.

2 Costs are underestimated, for similar emotional reasons. In this case, however, it is easier to blame someone else (i.e., the suppliers) for the missed budget.

3 Someone has forgotten to seasonally adjust the figures. Or someone has seasonally adjusted the figures when there was no need.

Beating budgets and other tricks

Any meeting where budgets, forecasts or accounts are discussed inevitably represents a solid opportunity for some hard-core bluffing. The nebulous nature of accounting means that the right set of questions is all that is needed to create an illusion of intelligence and understanding. Inevitably, no-one at the meeting will know the right answer, even the accountants that produced the report, which creates a fertile bluffer's territory. Basic techniques include:

> **66 The nebulous nature of accounting means that the right set of questions is all that is needed to create an illusion of intelligence. 99**

- Checking the additions, so you can ask about the anomalies that result.

- Asking (if any report descends into a morass of numbers), what they mean in plain words, and going on asking.

- Checking the dates. A surprising number of documents do not bear dates. Busy accountants occasionally issue last month's figures if they are putting together a package at midnight. Everybody will be grateful if you save them from asking fatuous questions about a wholly irrelevant set of figures.

- In a multi-company environment, asking which company or divisional grouping is covered if this is not clearly specified – for the same reason.

- In a review meeting, asking the presenter to review the highlights. This buys time and may also achieve explicit disclosures not evident, or present, in the text.

- Checking by enquiry, mental arithmetic, or calculator, whether the key ratios are the same as for the previous period. Asking diffidently about the ones that are not, as if the matter may be beneath them and you.

- Asking the presenter if he or she has any indication of different trends since the period covered by the report. This is a good idea for two reasons. First, it is not unknown for a group of articulate senior managers to sit in uncomplaining silence, even though each knows that recent events have made the paperwork obsolete, because each has a very good reason for keeping quiet. Second, it gives you the chance to venture into territory unsupported by text or hard fact, where your questions sound doubly credible because there are no facts to discredit them.

> **❝ It gives you the chance to venture into territory unsupported by text or hard fact. ❞**

- Asking the presenter what conclusions you are supposed to draw. This is not as naïve as it sounds. Put blandly it can sound very professional, not least because most accountants will have omitted to provide a summary or recommendation and will hate you for this.

All's fair in love, war and profit reporting.

ACCOUNTANTS

Qualified accountants fall into two broad groups; those that work in practice (an accountancy firm of some description) and those that work in industry (a company or similar organisation). They are all known as 'members' because to be an accountant you need to be a member of an accountancy institute. Accountants have been addressed as 'members' for entirely different reasons from time to time, but that's another story.

Given the overall image of accountants and their general perception as social pariahs (thank you, *Monty Python*), you may expect them to stick together and unite against the world. Not so. The reality is that rivalry, suspicion and insults abound within this sanctum. Accountants in practice don't generally get on with those in industry. Accountants in industry think those in practice are overpaid buffoons whose one aim in life is to stop them doing their job. Certified accountants loathe chartered accountants and aren't particularly fond of management accountants. Management accountants don't get on with anyone. Chartered accountants usually of think themselves as above everyone, but this doesn't stop them denigrating the other institutes, or even chartered accountants from other institutes. In this field, one should never expect grown-up behaviour among professionals.

> 66 Given the overall image of accountants you may expect them to stick together and unite against the world. Not so. The reality is that rivalry, suspicion and insults abound within this sanctum. 99

Members in practice

The accountancy profession refers to those who, after qualification, remain in the public practice firms (rather like schoolboys who go back to the old school as masters as soon as they've finished university) as 'members in practice'. They come in all shapes and sizes – the firms, that is, not the people – but there are four basic groups:

1 The smallest is the sole practitioner, a breed of which the Institutes quietly disapprove because, when they fall ill, there is no back-up. So they tend to damage the reputation of the profession as a whole. They will either be specialists at a high level, in tax perhaps, or generalists with clients who bring them a plastic bag bulging with receipts on 25th January

> **"It is inadvisable to invite a sole practitioner to a dinner party between October and February."**

every year and expect them to produce an accurate tax return. For this reason it is inadvisable to invite a sole practitioner to a dinner party between October and February – they will either fall asleep or rant about Her Majesty's Revenue and Customs, their clients, or both.

2 The small firm, with two to eight partners, probably generalist but with no large clients.

3 The medium-sized firms, with around 20–40 partners. These used to be the mainstay of the profession, big enough to be competent all-rounders but still of a size to be intimate and

with a clear identity. Alas, many of them have been swallowed by one of the majors or joined with another firm of similar size and usually achieved the worst of both worlds. Those that remain have sought to find a 'niche' that sets them apart from the masses. When they are not desperately searching for a niche, these firms are looking for a novel way to argue that they can offer a better service to their clients than the larger firms (which, to be fair, they often can).

4 The Big Four, which used to be the Big Six, and then the Big Five. They are big, and have merged with each other to become even bigger. Their entire raison d'être is based around size which, as we all know, is not always a sound inducement.

The firms are ranked by the total fee income they earn from their clients during the year. This figure is invented by the firms, largely unaudited and occasionally fictional. If you are uncertain about where a particular firm lies in the ranking, note carefully how they describe the top end of the profession, and their position:

- 'Probably the largest' means they are number two
- 'In the Big Four' means they are number four

– 'In the top 10' means number 10
– 'In the top 24' means 21 through 24.

Accountancy services

Irrespective of their size, firms will offer the same basic services to their clients. Most professions have a love/hate relationship with their clients. Accountancy is no exception, except that clients are compelled by law to use accountants, for audits at least, and are therefore even less gracious than they might be in a free market.

The climate varies directly with the financial results. If the accountants save or make money for the clients, all is well. If they merely cost money the atmosphere is neutral. If they lose money or are

> **"Clients are compelled by law to use accountants, for audits at least, and are therefore even less gracious than they might be in a free market."**

perceived as too expensive, the relationship tends to deteriorate rapidly.

It is necessary to examine the services the profession provides to clients to understand where these problems can arise. They fall into five main categories:

1 The core product is the **audit**. Nearly all audits are done because statute or custom demands. Hardly any are at the victims' choice but few cause

67

problems. The few that do cause problems usually hit the headlines (q.v. auditor liability).

2 **Book-keeping** and **accountancy** services come next, often hand-in-hand with the obligatory audit. Little potential for disaster here, except for a handful of unfortunate, if entertaining, cases.

3 **Tax work** follows inexorably. This is the problem area. People and companies hate paying tax. They also hate accountants who fail to prevent such payments. This is often because they fail to recognise the difference between compliance and planning.

Compliance is the business of computing and negotiating tax liabilities after the event. This is the area where most clients expect accountants to have a dramatic impact. They often do, but the impact is frequently a nasty shock, as the upright accountant has to point out that the tax consequences of the 'event' are highly unfavourable and, without fraudulent retrospective manipulation, cannot be improved. This is why, for those with foresight, tax planning is so popular and, for those without foresight, visionary accountants are in demand.

> **People and companies hate paying tax. They also hate accountants who fail to prevent such payments.**

Tax planning is usually regarded as a formal

process of consultation before the event, or the tax year, or the accounting year. In practice, it is a hectic and continuing process during which the accountants (in-house and external) desperately try to find out if a taxable event is about to happen so that they may:

- prevent it
- diminish it
- time it properly
- structure it properly
- move it offshore
- make it a non-event for tax purposes, or
- complement it with an event attracting tax relief.

The all-time great tax planners are not those who invent complex schemes, sailing closer to the wind than an Olympic dinghy helmsman. These schemers tend to spend a lot of time arguing precedents in court and also have their homes, offices, dustbins and mistresses raided by crack teams of Revenue investigators in combat gear. Instead, the greats beaver away quietly, deferring, offsetting and minimising the tax profile of the chargeable events and moving them into a lower tax bracket. This

> **" The all-time great tax planners are not those who invent complex schemes, sailing closer to the wind than an Olympic dinghy helmsman. "**

earns no OBEs but it avoids jail and makes the clients quite happy. It also prevents the Revenue flagging the clients' records for special attention next year.

4 Insolvency. Insolvency departments aid and administer companies before and after they discover they are broke (or someone else discovers it). It is important, and will make you very popular, to be able to point out that insolvency departments save more companies than they terminate. For this reason many firms take the glass-is-half-full approach and refer to the service as 'corporate recovery'.

5 Consultancy. This is the area where many firms make the most profits, so much so that many consultants have become wise to this fact and have set up their own consultancy practices, in order that they no longer have to share their hard-earned profits with other, less successful departments. Consultants are rarely qualified accountants and spend their time telling management how to do a job that they have never done themselves. They are able to convince companies to pay a lot of money for this service because they have MBAs and wear expensive suits.

These five areas represent a seemingly endless source of work for accountancy firms. However, a view has gathered momentum that if auditors of a company also carry out other, non-audit work for the same company, the moral integrity of the audit could be in doubt. As a result, auditors are limited in the non-audit work they can carry out for the same client. This is why auditors are generally miserable people.

The organisational structure

'Structure' and 'organisation' here are used in the ironic sense because it is a feature of most accountancy firms (particularly the larger ones) that while there is inevitably a structure, there is rarely organisation. Just as cobblers' children are the worst shod, the practice of management in accountancy firms differs somewhat from the practice of management in mainstream business. Not to put too fine a point on it, management is often conspicuous by its absence.

> **" It is a feature of most accountancy firms (particularly the larger ones) that while there is inevitably a structure, there is rarely organisation. "**

Accountants have been trained to be accountants, not managers, and if they stay in public practice have little or no exposure to good examples of modern methods. A few key examples may help demonstrate this:

- Decisions are made by committee with no one individual responsible for key areas. Hence, people tend to be against things rather than for them.

- Telling clients how to manage their business properly is more fun than managing one's own firm.

- No-one will pay you £300 and upwards per hour for managing your own firm.

- Any training which is unrelated to the task of extracting money from the clients is generally either considered low priority or is non-existent.

- Any employees that do not directly earn fees from clients (known as 'support staff') are often treated as second-class citizens and end up resenting the fee-earning accountants. Since this category includes catering staff it is not advisable to accept an offer of an in-house lunch from an accountancy firm.

"Some members of the profession actually believe their own propaganda and think they know everything on the day they qualify."

These symptoms are probably at their worst in accountancy because some members of the profession actually believe their own propaganda and think they know everything on the day they qualify.

Something all firms are keen on, however, is career and management structure. All firms have a clearly identifiable hierarchy, which dictates the level of salary and respect each employee can expect.

At the top of the tree are the partners. Within this group, though, there is another hierarchy. There will normally be a senior partner who may or may not be in charge, in that his authority is shared or usurped by a committee (variously known as the policy committee, management committee or wrecking crew). This is because the senior partner is either very democratic or incompetent.

> **Since the senior partner is elected by the partnership, these partners spend a lot of time ensuring that they are on the best possible terms with each other.**

Below the senior partner is a layer of full partners, all vying for the top job. Since the senior partner is elected by the partnership, these partners spend a lot of time ensuring that they are on the best possible terms with each other. Slightly less important are the junior partners, who are younger and therefore less disillusioned. Salaried partners have the title but no profit sharing rights and no financial responsibility if the firm is sued for negligence. They are generally very happy people.

Other members of the top echelons include various consultants, who are usually former senior partners who will not go away, and directors, so called because they are not qualified accountants and therefore cannot be admitted to the partnership. They have skills that are indispensable to the partnership and are likely to be both brighter and better rewarded than the average partner.

> **"The range of qualified staff is directly related to whether the firm relies on status in order to disguise poor pay or lack of partnership prospects."**

Below this heavy layer of management lies a wide tranche of qualified staff. The range of qualified staff is directly related to whether the firm relies on status in order to disguise poor pay or lack of partnership prospects. In a firm with particularly poor pay and prospects, this layer could include senior managers, junior managers, managers, assistant managers and, of course, trainees. Trainees may be described as 'students' or 'articled clerks', depending on the age of the partner addressing them. If the partner uses the latter term he is very near retirement.

The final level are known as support staff and because they do not earn fees from clients, are treated in many cases as a necessary evil.

Members in industry

The ultimate aim for any accountant working in

industry is a seat on the board as Finance Director or, in some hallowed cases, Chief Executive Officer. This means that they get to make strategic decisions, which is rather like driving someone else's top-of-the-range Mercedes for the first time, and you are also awarded share options and performance-related bonuses, which allows you to buy a mansion and an expensive education for each of your ungrateful children.

> **66 They get to make strategic decisions, which is rather like driving someone else's top-of-the-range Mercedes for the first time. 99**

Below the FD there will be several layers of accountants, all vying for the FD's job. These could include a Chief Accountant or a Financial Controller. If a company has both Chief Accountant and Controller, history probably imposed the latter over the former, who will now be sitting in a back room ticking off the days to his pension and mumbling quietly.

On the same level as the Controller you may also find a Treasurer, if the company has substantial money opportunities (or problems, as they used to be called) and wishes to hedge its bets about money – or about the succession to the financial directorship.

Career progression in the finance function is usually pretty good. There are several reasons for this:

a   If things go right as a result of the FD's work he or she gets the top job or a wider commercial role.

b   If things go badly wrong the FD gets fired.

c   Only the FD has a complete overview of the company's affairs and is thus a safe bet as successor if the CEO falls under a bus.

d   Good FDs get headhunted.

All these events enable the Controller to participate in the game of musical chairs, unless the Treasurer has been coming up fast on the inside.

> **66** Observe the frequency with which people venture beyond the confines of the finance offices. The most regular travellers will be the real accountants. **99**

If you have dealings with any organisation's finance staff it is also important to know who actually monitors and influences what goes on in the organisation as a whole, and who are merely bean-counters. Fortunately job titles tend to be reasonable indicators, except in the sort of company which is too apolitical or too small to have definitive titles.

For cases where the title doesn't help, observe the frequency with which people venture beyond the confines of the finance offices. The most regular travellers will be the real accountants.

The key job titles have changed over the years. Once, it was the 'cost accountant' who found out what the numbers meant. Then there was a brief period when the 'budget accountant' meant something, followed by a long run for 'management accountants' before the vogue for 'financial analysts' as the sharp end of the team. Any company using the older titles is also telling you something about itself.

> **In a new wave company it is vital to have a title that omits the word 'accountant'. Inventing a good title for a new job is more than half the battle.**

Your chances of promotion are affected not only by your merits but by your job title and in a new wave company it is vital to have a title that omits the word 'accountant'. Inventing a good title for a new job is more than half the battle.

Accountancy qualifications

Although we do not advise turning yourself into a replica of a qualified accountant, there may be occasions when you wish to hint that you've had some relevant training at some time in the past. For this you can choose the body most relevant to your past, or change your past to fit the qualification.

Accountants are usually members of one of the six recognised institutes ('usually' because some –

turf accountants, for instance – are not). Each institute has its own distinct and recognisable characteristic:

The Institute of Chartered Accountants in England and Wales (ICAEW) The best of the bunch, or so they would have one believe. Students of the institute spend three years training with an accountancy firm and if they pass they become chartered accountants, with a licence to audit or move into a senior finance role in industry. Either route will enable them to charge an eye-watering hourly rate.

The Institute of Chartered Accountants of Scotland (ICAS) As above, only with a sexier accent.

The Institute of Chartered Accountants in Ireland (ICAI) As above, only with considerably more charm.

The Chartered Association of Certified Accountants (ACCA) This is the largest institute, thanks to the many thousands of overseas members. In fact, there are concerns that the ACCA intends to take over the world, such is the extent and spread of its training programme. Chartered accountants would have you believe that the ACCA qualification is for people who aren't intelligent enough for the ICAEW or ICAS, or not Irish enough for the ICAI. This is by no means true, but it has left certified accountants with a lasting inferiority complex (and hence their reliance on comfort in numbers).

The Chartered Institute of Management Accountants (CIMA) The accountancy equivalent of graduates of the University of Life. The namby-pamby world of training in practice firms is not for them – they learn on the job and take their exams while working full time in a proper company. As a result, management accountants can actually do what auditors have only read about. Hardly surprising, then, that auditors and management accountants rarely see eye-to-eye.

The Chartered Institute of Public Finance and Accountancy (CIPFA) Underpaid beings who apply their skills to hospitals and other useful public institutions (and government departments, which could rarely be described as useful). Generally ignored by the rest of the accountancy profession, and so well worth championing in every way.

A BRIEF HISTORY OF COUNTING

Accounting is almost as old as civilisation itself. There is evidence that in the year 4000 BC the income generated by temples in Mesopotamia was written down. However, the origins of modern accounting are Italian. Curiously, given the reputation of their country for a slap-dash approach to many things (most notably driving), early Italian merchants were incredibly neat and ordered – often to the point of obsession and social ostracism – when it came to recording their transactions.

> **The origins of modern accounting are Italian. Curiously, given the reputation of their country for a slap-dash approach, early Italian merchants were incredibly neat and ordered.**

There is no reason why anyone should ever need to know this, but the oldest surviving example of written accounts (although not, sadly, double entry book-keeping, which was developed around 200 years later) dates from 1211, in the accounts of a client of a Florentine bank. If you are very keen, you can see full surviving examples of accounts books in one museum that date from 1300.

These early accounts usually consisted of three columns over a page, beginning with the name of the debtor or creditor in the left hand column, followed by 'shall give' or 'shall have' (in Italian, obviously) with a short description of the transaction in the middle column, and the amount in the last column. Once a debt was paid, a new sentence was written, substituting the phrase 'has given', 'have gotten' or 'we have given'. It was to take just 700 years and Bill Gates to develop this method into the modern-day spreadsheet.

Over the years, the three-column method gradually developed into a two-column structure, on the more logical basis that debits and credits could then be matched together. It has also been suggested that the double-entry method was a result of the Italian merchants' development of a more capitalist, profit-oriented way of thinking.

> **66** The man credited with the unforgettable title of the 'father of double entry book-keeping' (his mother must have been so proud) is Luca Pacioli, an Italian monk. **99**

The man credited with the unforgettable title of the 'father of double entry book-keeping' (his mother must have been so proud) is Luca Pacioli, an Italian monk, who described the method in great detail in his book *Summa di Arithmetica*, published in Venice in 1494. Just over 40 years later, another rip-roaring read was published in Antwerp: *Nieuwe Instructie ende dewijs der looffelijcker consten des rekenboecks* by Jan Ympyn Christoffels. Mercifully, the book was translated into English a couple of years later.

In 1553, double-entry book-keeping was introduced in the U.K. when the King's printer, Richard Grafton, published a work by James Peel, snappily entitled *The Maner and fourme how to kepe a perfecte reconyng, after the order of debitour and creditour*.

The translation of this early accounting theory into a full-blown and over-paid profession of accountants took a little longer. The first working accountants began appearing in Europe in the late 1700s and in 1831 the Bankruptcy Act mentioned accountants as being properly skilled to conduct audits, along with merchants and bankers. (It is a sign of the times that the idea of a banker conducting an audit today would be met with hoots of laughter.)

66 In 1831 the Bankruptcy Act mentioned accountants as being properly skilled to conduct audits, along with merchants and bankers. (It is a sign of the times that the idea of a banker conducting an audit today would be met with hoots of laughter.) 99

The first signs of accountancy as a lucrative, if slightly dull, profession came in 1842 when the Relief of Insolvent Debtors Act stipulated that any debtor owing less than £300 should attach a statement of debts when petitioning the Bankruptcy Court. The age of accountants making a living from the misfortune of others had begun.

GLOSSARY

Accounting policies Methods of accounting applied by a company that can be altered in order to produce more favourable results.

Amortisation Essentially the same as depreciation, but applied to intangible assets rather than fixed assets. The distinction between the two is often set as a trap for qualified accountants, let alone bluffers.

Audit trail Evidence that (in theory) everyday accounting processes leave behind, which can be checked and verified by the auditor.

Book value Value placed on an asset or liability for accounting purposes that bears no relation to its true worth.

Budgeting An exercise where the unknowledgeable force the unwilling to predict the impossible based entirely on the inaccurate.

Consolidated accounts System of accounting where all the mess is collected together in one statement in the hope that sheer size and complexity will dissuade anyone from reading it.

Contingent liability A debt that is dependent on the occurrence of a particular event, usually the ability to successfully persuade the auditor that the event will not happen.

Credit Something accountants rarely get.

Creditors Individuals or companies from whom you have acquired goods, services or loans for which you have yet to pay. These credits are considered to be current liabilities in your accounts (which will generally only get paid when your debtors' 'liabilities' have become real assets).

Current asset Cash and easily saleable equipment and stock that company executives can plunder if the going gets really tough.

Current liability Debts that the company has no intention of repaying within one year if it can possibly avoid it.

Debtors Individuals or companies who owe you money. These debts are considered to be current assets in your accounts (unless they are severely in debt, in which case they're a liability).

Deferred taxation Taxation that the company would like to think it does not owe, but does.

Equity In theory, the share of the company's assets that is owned by the shareholders. In practice, the shareholders will be last in line for a payout if the company goes under, just behind the chairman's plastic surgeon.

Exceptional item Any expense the auditor is willing to believe is outside the normal course of business.

Extraordinary item Used to mean very ordinary expenses such as restructuring costs but now means really extraordinary expenses, such as the cost of clearing up after an alien invasion.

FIFO 'First in first out', a method of valuing stock. Also a method never applied when accountancy firms are considering redundancies.

Going concern A company that is likely to survive until the next accounting period, unless the auditors have missed something really huge.

Goodwill Concept invented to explain the difference between the value of a company and the price another company paid for it.

Insolvency Bad news for the shareholders and employees; excellent news for the insolvency practitioner.

Intangible asset An asset that cannot be seen or felt and therefore is impossible to value (not that that fact has ever stopped an accountant).

Inventory American stock.

LIFO 'Last in first out', a method of valuing stock. Also, a policy frequently applied when accountancy firms are considering redundancies.

Liability Money or goods owed by a company. Also, a first-year audit trainee.

Materiality The level below which errors are considered not to matter. In theory, the concept of materiality is supposed to consider many factors and the context of the error. In practice it is an arbitrary percentage of profit, as high as the accountant believes he can get away with.

Off balance sheet Mysterious place where all assets or liabilities that companies don't want to acknowledge end up. Not always, but sometimes, Spain.

Petty cash Source for all dubious expenses claims.

Prudence A fundamental accounting principle, designed to lend dignity to inaccuracy.

Reconciliation The art of proving that one inaccurate figure exactly agrees with another inaccurate figure.

THE AUTHORS

Liz Fisher grew up in a small town in South Wales, where so little happened that a career in accountancy seemed like a tremendously exciting option.

A writer from an early age, she planned to study English at university but thanks to an impossibly obscure question about John Keats wound up doing accountancy instead.

On graduation, eschewing the glamorous salary and lifestyle double-entry had promised, she joined *Accountancy* magazine, where she spent 10 happy years writing authoritatively about the many things she had failed to understand. A freelance journalist and writer, she lives in Stratford Upon Avon. She still gives Keats a wide berth.

John Courtis is a Chartered Accountant. His experience of accountancy gained in public practice, the Royal Air Force and Ford Motor Company led him to leave accounting behind a great many years ago and become a headhunter.

He owns a number of odd cars and eccentric cameras, has absolutely no sporting interests and dislikes most indoor games except those he can win. These include Trivial Pursuits, draughts and liar dice.

Bond

In persuading people of the books' superiority over the films, concentrate on the nature of his character. Quote a gem from Fleming's pen to illustrate your point, such as: 'Regret was unprofessional – worse, it was death-watch beetle in the soul.'

Management

Getting a simple message across a large department accurately is in truth quite difficult. People read what they want to believe, hear what they want to hear and generally behave like aliens who have not fully mastered English and do not plan to.

Golf

Well-meaning but over-loud cries of "Do you want the flag out or tended?" can easily disrupt concentration. Most telling of all, the apparently friendly "Tricky length that" or "Quite a bit of golf there yet". Putting is entirely in the mind. On a bad day even the best can be persuaded to miss.

Consultancy

Always be hard to get. A blank diary must be made to seem full. Bogus meetings must be cancelled or postponed. You must always appear to have had to tear yourself away from urgent and important matters to attend to your client's needs.

Economics

Achieving the multifarious objectives of economic policy-making (high growth, zero unemployment, minimal borrowing and low inflation) can be likened to that infuriating game with a number of tiny silver balls that have to be manoeuvred into shallow holes.

Quantum Universe

Never commit yourself about the outer limits of the Universe or the quantum realm even to a 'probably'. Anything you utter with certainty, or declare to be 'probably true' could return to haunt you and, it can be said with confidence, probably will. If you know what's good for you, a 'possibly' is the farthest you will go.

Comments on other titles

Archaeology:

"Unmissable! Indispensable for old and new archaeologists alike, this is a fabulous book! Having been involved in this bizarre pastime for some years myself, it made me howl with recognition."   Reader from Sheffield

The Flight Deck:

"An excellent light-hearted look at the operations on the flight deck and a great insight into how it all works. Amusing and informative."   Reader from Leeds

Marketing:

"Any marketing person who has not read this book has almost certainly wasted their time and money reading all the others. It's funny, witty, and true."   Reader from London

Cricket:

"A great gift for cricket widows (as we're called) for an introduction to cricket but also for its players and lovers for its funny take on the game."   Reader from Liverpool

"Everything you need to know about the major composers with all the right things to say. Extremely witty and well written."

Reader from Los Angeles

ᵗʰᵉBluffer's® Guides

TITLE	QUANTITY	TITLE	QUANTITY
Accountancy	....	Middle Age	....
Archaeology	....	Music	....
Astrology	....	Negotiation	....
Banking		Opera	....
Bond	....	Paris	....
The Classics	....	Philosophy	....
Computers	....	Public Speaking	....
Consultancy	....	The Quantum	
Cricket	....	Universe	....
Divorce	....	Relationships	....
Doctors	....	Rugby	
Economics	....	Seduction	
Flight Deck	....	Sex	....
Football	....	The Simpsons	
Genetics	....	Skiing	
Golf	....	Small Business	....
Jazz	....	Stocks & Shares	....
Law	....	Teaching	
Life Coaching	....	University	....
Management	....	Whisky	....
Marketing	....	Wine	....
Men	....	Women	....

Ⓞ
Oval Books
5 St John's Buildings Canterbury Crescent London SW9 7QH

We like to hear from our readers.
Please send us your views on our books
and we will publish them as appropriate on
our web site: ovalbooks.com.

Oval Books also publish the best-selling
Xenophobe's Guide® series –
see www.ovalbooks.com

Both series can be bought via Amazon or directly
from us, Oval Books through our web site
www.ovalbooks.com or by contacting us.

Oval Books charges the full cover price
for its books (because they're worth it) and
£2.00 for postage and packing on the first
book. Buy a second book or more and postage
and packing will be entirely FREE.

To order by post please fill out the accompanying
order form and send to:
Oval Books
5 St John's Buildings
Canterbury Crescent
London SW9 7QH

cheques should be made payable to: Oval Books

or phone us on +44 (0)20 7733 8585
or visit our web site at: www.ovalbooks.com

Payment may be made by Visa or Mastercard and orders are
dispatched as soon as the card details and mailing address are
received. If the mailing address is not the same as the card holder's
address it is necessary to give both.

Oval Books